Church Split

Surviving the
Perfect Storm

Church Split

Surviving the Perfect Storm

by

Pastor Art Rivers

Word of His Mouth Publishers
Mooresboro, NC

All Scripture quotations are taken from the **King James Version** of the Bible.

ISBN: 978-1-941039-37-3
Printed in the United States of America
©2023 Pastor Art Rivers

Word of His Mouth Publishers
Mooresboro, NC
www.wordofhismouth.com

Table of Contents

Introduction

A person who has not been a pastor can never really grasp just how fully a man's life becomes intertwined with his ministry. It is like a cancer that wraps around every vital organ, every blood vessel, every artery, every cell of the body. To try and separate the two is nearly impossible without killing the host. This is not to say that it is an unpleasant thing. Unlike cancer, the ministry is actually life rather than death! The one suffering from cancer spends every day wondering how he can be cured of it. The man in the pastorate does not want to be "cured"; he wants to be a little more "infected" every day. The ministry is a calling, but it is also an addiction:

1 Corinthians 16:15 *I beseech you, brethren, (ye know the house of Stephanas, that it is the firstfruits of Achaia, and that they have **addicted themselves to the ministry** of the saints,)*

I developed this addiction as a kid preacher just a few weeks away from graduating from seminary when God opened the door for me to become a pastor. It was a small church in a small town, and everyone in it was old. But none of that mattered to me in the least. To me, it may as well have been the Metropolitan Tabernacle, and I went into the task with the full vigor and enthusiasm of youth, certain that I would change not just that town for the glory of God but the entire world.

I am older now; much older, in fact. Gray at the temples is starting to replace the dark hair of my youth. I still smile a lot, but it is a smile that is tempered with long years of experience in battles that I never imagined I would have, chief among which was a particularly brutal church split.

And yet, I am as thrilled to be in the ministry now as I was the very first day.

I survived. My family survived. The church survived. All of the above are actually stronger and more enjoyable than ever.

I said that to say this. If you are going through or have been through a church split, life isn't over. It isn't necessarily even permanently damaged. In fact, not only can you survive, you can be better for the experience; we serve a God who makes beautiful things out of broken things.

Hopefully, this recounting of my experience can help to make that possible for you.

Pastor Art Rivers

Chapter 1
Soft Winds Blowing

Acts 27:13 *And when the south wind blew softly...*

The term "honeymoon period" is a really good one to describe what the early days of a first pastorate are generally like. Like a real marriage, the honeymoon time for church and pastor is generally when, though everything is still very much not perfect, both sides are in love and willing to be patient with the other.

And boy, did my church and I need that honeymoon period.

Old. Respectable. Well-financed. Upper crust. All of that was the church on the "nicer" side of our small town. Our church, though, was exactly like that, except that it was completely different in every regard. It was the "other church" in town, the one that had not been around for generations. It was looked down on. There was very little money in the bank. Most everyone who attended was, rather than upper crust, more like "cheap pot-pie crust."

As for me, I was the newly married kid preacher with more zeal than knowledge.

But somehow, the church and I got along really well, and God quickly began to bless.

We went out into the community and knocked on doors, and people came to visit the church. From the moment I got there, we started working on the grounds and facilities, trying to make an old, run-down building look a bit more palatable to potential visitors and members. And boy, did we have the work to do! Through years of neglect, the place really was in shambles. It had the typical 1950s paneling on all of the walls, and the flooring was entirely a wreck. The roof leaked. The paint on the exterior of the building was clearly chosen and applied by either a drug-addled homeless painter using whatever colors he could come up with by mixing everything he had together or the most sadistic committee in the history of mankind.

It was gloriously, beautifully hideous, and even downright unsafe in many ways.

But the wonderful thing about starting in that type of horrible setting is that everything you do to improve it is amazing and exciting.

Things like white paint inside and out. Things like new, bargain carpet. Things like re-shingling the roof with factory seconds that were still a million times better than what was on there to begin with. And little by little, the old building began to take on a decidedly "respectable" air about it.

We managed to get rid of the ancient old seating and get some new-to-us pews. We renovated the Sunday school wing. We made the kitchen into something that health inspectors no longer felt the need to wear hazmat suits into.

And people began to fill the place up. Better still, people started getting saved, getting baptized, becoming true followers of Christ, and going out and telling others what Jesus had done for them and where. Within a few short years, our church was becoming pretty well known as a growing, vibrant place—a place that was truly alive. The finances improved dramatically, so much so that we started taking on missionaries for support. And then musicians and singers started showing up. Some had just moved to town and were looking for a church just like ours. Others had gotten saved and wanted to use their talents for the Lord that they had previously used for the devil.

All the while, I had been bi-vocational; the church was only able to pay me a very tiny amount when I first came due to the finances being so very limited. But finally, even that changed. We had to tighten our personal budget a good bit, but the church took me on as a full-time pastor. I was ridiculously thrilled; now, not only could I pour way more time and effort into the work, I could also go to fellowships with other pastors in the area!

Into all of that happiness, the good God of heaven one day decided to pour out even more into my life. I came home from the church to our tiny house one afternoon, and Elizabeth asked me to please sit down. The tone of voice she used was different, very different than any she had ever used before with me; I really could not decipher what it meant and where the conversation was headed. Did she have cancer, or had some distant uncle died and left her a huge inheritance?

"Honey, you have been a wonderful husband," she began, "but it is time for you to expand your responsibilities."

I was drawing a complete blank. Where in the world was this headed? Did I need to do more laundry or dishes? Maybe be quicker about the trash duty? And why do women always have to be so cryptic? Is this something God built into their DNA, or is this a product of the fall?

She just stared at me and then broke into a million-watt grin.

"You are going to be a father."

Nine months later, our church had a youth group of one, our son, Winston.

Chapter 2
Well On Our Way

Acts 27:13 *And when the south wind blew softly,* ***supposing that they had obtained their purpose...***

The early years had their waves, just like any voyage, but on the whole, they were very pleasant and successful years. It truly seemed like we had "obtained our purpose" or were at least well on our way. And that is saying something, considering the reality of our situation. When I first stepped onto the property as the pastor, the church had nothing. The town itself was and still is exceedingly small. And then there is an inevitable fact that when a tiny church in a tiny town gets a new pastor, the news seems to attract every crazy person for miles around!

I remember well one of our first. She had been involved with a gang when she was a teenager. In the midst of a "disagreement" with a rival gang, she was beaten severely and spent months in a coma before finally coming out of it. But that kind of a thing will definitely render a person "less than lucid." She saw aliens. She heard voices. She was incredibly paranoid. She once chewed out our ladies for throwing away old potato salad. It had been in the refrigerator for months; anyone who tried to eat it would have either died or become a hideous mutant of some sort. So our ladies cleared it and many other things out on a Saturday workday. But she was utterly convinced that it was her potato salad being jettisoned and that it was being done to hurt her feelings! She later called the authorities, I kid you not, to report that our church was "harboring terrorists." Those "terrorists" were a lovely couple from Jordan who had both lived in America since infancy and were Bible-believing Christians, patriotic Americans, and had never been in trouble with the law a day in their lives.

When she later left the church, I had some ladies come to me and ask if I would like them to try and get her back in. Without a moment's hesitation, I shouted, "NO! Don't you dare!"

But we were not to be rid of her so easily. Some months later, she called and asked me and my wife to come by and bring her back to church. Reluctantly, we went and picked her up. When we did, she said, "Oh, pastor, thank you so much for sending that lady by to tell us how much you missed us. If you hadn't done that, I never would have come back." Perplexed beyond measure as to who would do such a thing, I asked her to describe the lady. When she did, I nearly wrecked the car; I knew the lady.

She wasn't a member of my church.

She was a deacon's wife at the church she had been going to since she left ours! That trollop had gone to her, pretending to be from my church and asking her to come back. Apparently, her craziness had driven them to desperate measures to be rid of her!

She was not the only one. There was also the guy with "tax issues." He and his girlfriend started coming to church and one day announced to me that they wanted to get married. I would not do the ceremony for reasons that I will not go into here, but I told him that if they were going to get married anyway, I would at least be willing to counsel them on some important issues of marriage. He really appreciated that and began coming to weekly counseling sessions. On one of those weeks, I began to cover finances and how to do a budget. It was then that I learned that he was involved in a "tax protest group," which refused to pay taxes because the government "does immoral things with that money." At this point, I was beginning to wonder if there was any sanity left on this side of the pond!

My jaw dropped. Slamming it back into place like a character from an old Saturday morning cartoon, I shrieked, "Listen to me very carefully: your friends are daft, and you are going to go to prison for listening to them!" I then proceeded to take my Bible and show him that Jesus Himself commanded us to pay our taxes. This was just one more instance of our church being an insanity magnet in my early days as a pastor! To his credit, this was a really good man, and he and I went to the tax office together and got things cleared up and set right.

The list could go on forever. There was the time that a lady visiting our church for the very first time went to the altar to deal with someone that we had been witnessing to for a good while. A visitor! This lady, before we could get to her, had done so much damage that the girl we had been witnessing to never came back.

There was the lady who was adamantly, vehemently opposed to allowing minorities to come to our church. I, of course, being the type who actually believes his Bible, was not going along with that for even a second. I ran a bus and picked up whoever would come, including a couple of precious black children. When I started bringing them, the woman developed some "obvious habits." Every service, we had a time to shake hands and fellowship, always at the same point in the service. The woman started getting up and going to the bathroom just a couple of minutes before the fellowship time, and she would stay in there until after it was over. What did I do? I started changing the order of service and having the fellowship time at unexpected moments. But the woman was not so easily defeated. Once she saw what I was doing, she started wearing gloves to church, gloves that came all the way up to her elbows!

With all of that going on, we still managed to see very good growth and very good progress throughout the early years. We ran buses. We knocked on doors. We handed out gospel tracts. We started a youth choir and a youth ministry.

That youth work was, and is, amazing. And the fact that we started it with only one child in church to go along with all of the long-established old people made it that much more a work of the Lord. With only that one boy, I told the church that we were going to have a youth meeting. They said, "But preacher, we don't have any children!" I said, "That's okay; let's have the meeting and see what happens."

We did. And that very first youth meeting, two precious children got saved! Their family joined the next day and is still with us all these years later.

And we grew. We grew to the point that we had to expand our facilities. And then we outgrew even that. It was every pastor's dream; take a small church whose chief problem is that it is dying member by member and see it transformed into a church whose chief problem is figuring out where to put everyone!

We really did seem to be well on our way.

Chapter 3
A New Harbor

Acts 27:12 *And because the haven was not commodious to winter in, the more part advised to depart thence also...* **13** *...loosing thence, they sailed close by Crete.*

There comes a point in a facility where every possible space has been utilized, every step of possible expansion taken, and there is simply no more room to grow. Our church reached that point. And yet, there was such a hesitancy on the part of some of the people, especially the old guard who had been there for decades, to be willing to do anything about it.

One Sunday morning, I gathered some of that old guard by the windows that faced out into the parking lot a few minutes before service.

"What do you need, Pastor?" one of them queried.

"What do you see?" I asked.

They all looked out into the parking lot, and one replied laconically, "Lots of cars."

I nodded.

"What do you not see?" I inquired.

One of them finally got it.

"There are no empty parking spaces."

"Correct," I said. "Now, just watch with me for a few minutes."

In the next couple of minutes, six cars pulled through our parking lot, saw that there were no spaces, and left.

The eyes of all of my men grew wide.

"This is happening every week," I said. "We need to do something, and we need to do something quickly."

That, in short, is how I ended up in my first building project as a young pastor.

We purchased a piece of property adjacent to the church, contacted an architect, and started making plans to build. This was brand new territory for all of us, but the people were really excited. We were going to have a new church building! We were also going to have a huge parking lot, something that people would not have to drive away from for lack of spaces.

And we did. A big, beautiful, yet reasonable facility, one that balanced needs and budget really well. And the day we walked in for our first service, we had visitors everywhere, many of whom stayed, became members, and are still with us to this day.

Our "new harbor" was a pleasant one. The air conditioners all worked, which was a wonderful change for us. The electrical system did not make one fear that someone could be electrocuted at any moment. The used but new to us pews were nonetheless nice and comfortable. The carpet was lovely. And there was not a single piece of paneling anywhere; everything was drywall and wood. And, perhaps best of all, there was enough bathroom capacity for everyone! More than once, in our old facility, we would have people leave, drive down the street to a store to use the bathroom, and then sometimes (but not always) come back for the rest of the service.

We also saw continued improvements in every aspect of the ministry and services. In the old church, our piano was an ancient and monstrous upright, one of those things that you can find listed free for the taking in any trade publication weekly in every town across America as long as you can find a dozen or so men with strong backs and weak minds to come pick it up.

In the new building, people were able to walk in to the sight and sound of a lovely baby grand piano.

The buses improved as well; the museum-level ancient school cheese wagons gave way to slightly less old and a bit more reliable vehicles with which to pick people up for church and take trips to wonderful places together.

And we grew yet again. Word was spreading that something good was happening at the little church out in Nowhereville. People started driving in for services from miles and miles away. We were having people from five counties show up regularly for worship!

The altars were in use at every single service. Rarely did more than a week or two go by without someone getting saved. The baptistery was constantly being filled. The choir grew. We took on even more missionaries. We hired more staff.

And the youth group continued to grow as well – both through evangelism and through "Riversism."

"Honey," Elizabeth sweetly said one day out of the blue, "What would be the odds on us doing a bit of work on the house sometime soon?"

Men, please learn a lesson here. Your wife rarely asks innocent questions; wife questions almost always are like the tip of the iceberg, hiding the gigantoiceblock just underneath the surface.

"What do you mean?" I asked warily.

"Our 'river' is going to get a bit deeper; you are going to be a father again."

Nine months later, our family and our church welcomed little Tara into the world. Winston was now a big brother, Elizabeth and I were now "tied with our opponents" for numerical superiority in the home, and we were as happy as if we had already gotten to heaven the day before.

Other children were coming along as well. As new, young couples joined the church, they brought their children, had more along the way, and our nurseries (two of them!) were filled to overflowing.

And then, just a year later...

"Sweetheart, do you really like where we live?"

What in the world?

If I remember correctly, I said something exceptionally profound in response, something like "Uhhhhh..."

Charles Dickens would have doubtless been proud.

"We don't have enough rooms," she said simply.

I am thick-headed, but given enough practice runs, I can usually eventually get something right.

"Are we having another one?" I asked.

She just grinned from ear-to-ear and hugged me really tightly. And I needed her to because, at that moment, I was absolutely panicking; we lived in a one thousand square foot house with two bedrooms, and we already had two itty-bitty children sharing the other bedroom! And my pastoral salary was definitely not going to allow us to buy something bigger anytime soon.

Nine months later, we welcomed little Anabeth into the world, into our church, and into the youth group. And, by building a wall that cut our living room in half, we came up with another tiny room for Winston so that Tara and Anabeth could have the other one as their "sister domicile." Winston was unfazed; he has always been laid back to the point of near catatonia.

So the church had its large new harbor, and we had a tiny new harbor in our tiny old harbor, and all of us were absolutely as happy as could be.

Chapter 4
The Perfect Storm

Acts 27:14 *But not long after there arose against it a tempestuous wind, called Euroclydon.*

Before Paul and company set sail, they had something pretty precious: a warning of the danger ahead.

Acts 27:9 *Now when much time was spent, and when sailing was now dangerous, because the fast was now already past, Paul admonished them,* **10** *And said unto them, Sirs, I perceive that this voyage will be with hurt and much damage, not only of the lading and ship, but also of our lives.*

Mind you, they ignored him, but at least they were given fair warning.

And that is where our church split, like those that many others have endured, was far worse; we had absolutely no warning of the storm that was barreling our way and would threaten to drown us all.

At this point, I should tell you that I am not going to do what many of my readers may wish for me to do. I am not going to re-litigate our split. I am not going to "name and shame" anyone. If I had written this book right after the split or even a few years after it, I most certainly would have. But enough years have passed by that God has soothed many of the hurts with His good grace. And we have also been blessed to have many of the people involved contact us and apologize for their part in the entire messy affair. In fact, while none of them are at our church anymore, we now once again count many of them as dear friends nonetheless.

But for the purposes of this book, we should get back to the storm.

I was no longer a young pastor. I was actually having children in the youth group make loving "Old-man" jokes about me! I did not and do not mind; life is way too short not to have a sense of humor.

I was also, though, something both wonderful and dangerous all at the same time: comfortable.

If you have ever pastored a church, you know that it is often one battle after another after another in rapid succession. They come like the waves of the sea, and the only appreciable difference is the size of each one. But then, sometimes, the most amazing thing happens; all of the waves lay down for an extended period of time.

I remember well what that felt like. After enduring so many battles and trials in the early years, we got to a place where there was hardly a ripple anywhere in sight.

Our church was bigger than ever. We had good music, we took great trips together, both the choir and the youth choir were full, and everyone was (at least on the surface) getting along really well. And financially, things were exceptionally good. For the first time ever, we were bringing in substantially more in tithes and offerings than was going out in bills each month. The treasury was swelling, and we were finally able to not make every decision based on "what is the cheapest possible option we can get by with?"

It felt really good.

And neither Elizabeth nor I had the slightest clue that Euroclydon was barreling our way.

It took a few years afterward for us to finally unravel all that happened and how long it had been brewing. A family that had been with us for a very long time had gotten into some things, things that required me as a pastor to confront them privately a year before the split. And that meeting, to put it mildly, did not go well at all. They blew up, screaming and shouting, and stormed out of my office, vowing never to set foot in our church again.

Three evenings later, they were back for Wednesday evening service and assured me that everything was hunky dory and that they were absolutely on board with us.

You have no idea how many times since then I have stared at myself in the mirror and said something like, "Hey, minister with the genius-level IQ; have I told you lately how stupid you were? It takes a certified moron not to have seen through that."

They were on board, alright; onboard like terrorists looking for a good place to plant the bomb.

For a year, they subtly went family to family, feeling them out and feeding them sly suggestions that perhaps it was time to "reign the pastor in." I will give the man credit; he was exceptionally good at what he did. After the split, he called one of my dearest and most faithful men, my treasurer, and spun a tail of lies and embezzlement dark enough to blot out the sun. He did not know that my treasurer was looking at the books and accounts as he spoke to him and could see that he was lying. When the phone call ended, my treasurer called me and told me all that the man had said. And then he said, "The bad news, Pastor, is that if I had not been looking at the books and accounts as he spoke, I would have believed every word he said. I can assure you, if he spins that tale for anyone else, they will believe him."

Like Absalom, he won the hearts of some of my very dearest people, and I never saw it coming. And when it all blew up, my jaw dropped as I watched two deacons, the choir leader, and four Sunday school teachers storm out together. I would have bet you every single dime I owned that all of those men and their families were absolutely loyal to me and confident in me. I was utterly blindsided.

And the damage was just beginning. The next few months were a constant battle for the hearts and minds of the remaining congregation, a battle that I was losing in epic fashion. Every service brought new empty spots in the pews, spots that had been filled by people I never imagined would leave. And, each time I tried to keep my heart from getting consumed in anger and hatred, each time I attempted to be longsuffering, a new taunt was lobbed our way by the main ringleaders. One that I will never forget is the taunt, "We took the tithers with us; we will bankrupt that church and see it shut down, and you run out of town."

The worst part of the pain, though, was having our three young children crawl onto the bed with us each night, sobbing their eyeballs out and asking, "Why do they all hate us? What did we do?" That was gut-wrenching; these were the only friends my church-born children had ever known. The young people that those families took with them were my children's heroes.

But no storm lasts forever, including ours. Eventually, with over forty percent of the church gone and with the lines between the stayers and the leavers finally firmly drawn, the wind stopped blowing, and all that was left was to start clearing the debris and attempting to survive.

Chapter 5
Preparing for the Storm

Without going into undue details, I have now told you about our church split, our perfect storm. But this book is not about the storm; it is about surviving the storm. So, at this point, I want to backtrack for your benefit to the years and months prior to the storm. You see, God was very good to help us do some things right without even realizing it, things that helped us to make it through! So you, Pastor, should pay attention at this point whether you fear a coming split or whether you think everything is perfect and you will never have to worry about that. And, for the pastor who is going though a split now or has come through one and whose survival is still in doubt, don't worry; I will be with you shortly, and I am bringing help with me.

I have spoken just a bit in generalities about our church finances prior to the split. But please allow me to give a few more helpful details.

When I was growing up, to paraphrase Gru from Despicable Me, "In terms of money, we had no money."

Zip. Zilch. Nada. Poor? We were so poor that I didn't even have any clothes until I was seven years old when my mother bought me a hat so that I could look out the window.

Okay, okay, that last part is hyperbole. But the poor part wasn't. And because I grew up poor, I learned 1) to do without things, and 2) how to do things, and 3) to treat every penny as precious. And I carried all of that into my adulthood and into the ministry.

In our early years at the church, it was not uncommon for someone to inform me that a toilet was leaking and that we needed to contact a plumber to come and fix it. It was also not uncommon for me to show up the next morning in grubby clothes, carrying tools, and fix the problem. The same thing applied to electrical issues and leaky roofs and sagging door frames. We saved a substantial amount of money by doing things ourselves rather than hiring professional help.

When it came time to build the church, we took the same approach. We did so much of the work ourselves that, based on two different contractors' estimates, we saved around $900,000 on the project.

We bought vans and buses to bring children to church. I lettered them myself.

Now, please don't get nervous; I am not telling you that you have to be a pastor/plumber/electrician/roofer/contractor to survive a church split. I am telling you, though, that many churches and pastors are pretty cavalier with finances during the good days and never lay up for some potential future storm. By the time our storm hit, our church had a substantial financial reserve to work with. That is one of the most essential things you can ever do ahead of time to make sure that you survive a split.

And we needed it. Our new building was large, and so was our monthly payment. When the main split-master boasted that they would shut us down using finances, he doubtless had that very thing in mind. But we went into the battle with a nice war chest, and that helped to stave off his worst hopes for us.

But it isn't just church finances that need to be considered ahead of time; a pastor's own finances are every bit as crucial, if not more so! If a pastor can be quickly starved out, he will leave the pasture, and the wolves will return for the sheep. And, once again, God was really good to let us do some things right ahead of time without us even being really aware of it.

My background in poverty taught me the value of saving for a rainy day, and it especially taught me the value of an emergency fund that one never touches except in a true, bonafide disaster.

Let me check, here, for a second...

Yes, a church split qualifies, especially when it means that you likely will not be getting paid for the foreseeable future.

Through the early years of our marriage, Elizabeth and I scrimped and saved without ever alarming the children. If you ever see her, ask her about the year I strode out into the woods and cut down a "Charlie Brown Christmas tree" for us instead of buying one off of the tree lot!

When I tell you we were miserly with ourselves, I mean it. We were generous with the church and with our children and with those in need, but we ourselves did without a lot because I was intent on hitting a particular goal.

And we did. A year before the storm descended on us, we closed the door to our little security safe, smiled, and said, "Five thousand dollars is not bad at all." And then we intentionally forgot that it even existed; our hope was for us to have it still on our death beds.

We do not have it anymore.

Don't worry, we have rebuilt a new one. But when the split hit, we were able to go home that night, look into each other's eyes, and say, "We and the children can eat tomorrow, and the day after that, and for a whole bunch of days after that. They may starve us out, but it won't be any time soon."

In the long years since we survived the split, the memories of all of that often comes flooding back at random times. And each time they do, I silently pray, "Thank you, Lord, for helping us to be ready for it."

Another pastor friend of mine had things go very differently for him. He was fifty-five years old and was pastoring a church for just three months when the storm hit. I called him and found that he had already resigned. I asked him how much of an emergency fund he had to work with, and his answer was, "Nothing; I don't have anything."

How does a person work all of their lives and yet not have anything when the storm hits? If necessary, you should live on beans and water for a few years until you have an emergency fund!

There was another component to our survival that predated the storm, and that was (and one must sound like Liam Neeson when one says these words) "a particular set of skills." Both Elizabeth and I were a bit different from the "Traditional Young Pastor's Family." In many TYPFs, the wife has exactly one skill, getting pregnant, and the husband has exactly one skill, pastoring. In our family, we both brought other skills into the marriage with us. You already know that I was capable of construction work. But I also had other valuable skills as well, as did Elizabeth, who was a capable accountant. So, when the split happened, both of us knew that even if I never drew another paycheck from the church, both of us had in-demand skills that could earn us a paycheck as long as needed.

Do you realize how sensible this is? Even the secular world grasps this concept. I give you Harrison Ford...

"Before he was Han Solo or Indiana Jones, Harrison Ford was a carpenter. In 1964, Ford moved to Hollywood to become an actor. 'But I arrived on a metaphoric bus full of people who had the same ambition,' he said. So he came up with this plan to prevail over the competition. As Ford spent time around the other aspiring actors on that metaphoric bus, he became aware of something:

"Most of them were in a hurry.

"They were in a hurry to 'make it' or to make lots of money or to prove something to someone. Whatever the reason, most were on a tight timeline. So Ford's plan was to do the opposite: to lengthen his timeline. To do so, Ford said, 'I had to have another source of income. So I became a carpenter.'

"'By doing carpentry,' he explained, 'I was able to wait it out. And as the years went by, the attrition rate eliminated many of those people from the competition pool until finally, there were only a few of us left on the bus from that entering class. I always saw life that way—you just have to find a way to stick it out, to prevail.'

"Ford chose carpentry for two reasons. First, when he first moved to Hollywood, he taught himself the basic carpentry skills needed to fix up his dilapidated house. He was immediately attracted to the process of fixing things, calling it 'a form of meditation.' Second, he thought—since Hollywood is an everybody-knows-everybody kind of town—a carpentry job could lead to an acting job.

"Indeed.

"Ford became known as the 'carpenter to the stars.' His roster of clients included Francis Ford Coppola, James Caan, Richard Dreyfuss, and Joan Didion. Most famously, in the early 1970s, Ford was building 'an elaborate portico entrance' at Coppola's offices where Coppola's friend, George Lucas, was leading casting meetings for Star Wars.

"One day, Ford said, 'I was asked by George if I would read with the other actors. There was no indication that I might be considered for a part in the film.'

" ' I read with about 300 actors, and weeks later, they asked me if I wanted to play Han Solo.'

"Ford's 'stick it out' strategy is a civilian version of what military strategists refer to as 'winning through attrition.' In a study of the major wars that shaped the course of history, the strategist and historian B.H. Liddell Hart found that only 2% of battles were won as a result of a direct attack. The majority of successful armies throughout history, Hart writes, all had the 'power of endurance to last.'

"As Ford put it, 'You just have to find a way to stick it out, to prevail.' "

(https://www.linkedin.com/posts/billy-oppenheimer-70612782_before-he-was-han-solo-or-indiana-jones-activity-70693052846277 30432-CRJA)

You may also be aware of another guy, a preacher, actually, who adopted this strategy of using marketable skills to survive the hard times in ministry:

Acts 18:1 *After these things Paul departed from Athens, and came to Corinth;* **2** *And found a certain Jew named Aquila, born in Pontus, lately come from Italy, with his wife Priscilla; (because that Claudius had commanded all Jews to depart from Rome:) and came unto them.* **3** *And because he was of the*

38

same craft, he abode with them, and wrought: for by their occupation they were tentmakers.

Paul. Paul the Apostle, the greatest minister who ever lived other than Christ Himself.

Paul the tentmaker. Paul the "Why, yes, I can absolutely make you a three-room tent complete with a nursery by next Wednesday" guy.

If I could give one piece of advice to every Bible college and seminary on earth, it would be to require every single student, in addition to their theological major, to have a marketable minor as well. If every student graduating from Bible college could exegete Scripture and fix plumbing leaks equally well, very few pastors would ever get starved out of a church.

So, let me ask you a question, Pastor. If, by chance, an unseen storm is heading your way, and if by chance it wallops you tomorrow and you end up with no paycheck from the church, do you have 1) an emergency fund and 2) any marketable skills? If the answer to either or both is no, then you have some work to do.

There are other considerations, though, to preparing for a split before it happens. I mentioned earlier that we lost two deacons, the choir leader, and four Sunday school teachers all at one time, not to mention the many others who went with them. And had all of the remaining people shown up week after week to no choir and four Sunday school classes without teachers, it would have been devastating. But the very first choir director under my pastorship had been... me. I took music in seminary, among other things. Now, as quickly as I could, I trained someone else to lead the choir because it is pretty unwise for a pastor to do everything. But since I knew how to do it, I called a choir practice the very next week after the split, and we picked up right where the former choir director had left off. And since Elizabeth and I are both capable teachers, we stepped into some of the now vacant class lecterns. We also had appointed a couple of assistant teachers for some of the classes in the months previous to the split, and they were able to step in and help as well, so no classes fell apart.

So, Pastor, before you ever have a split, be aware that the more you are capable of doing (both in and out of church), and the more backups you have in place, and the more emergency financial reserves you have in place, the more likely you are to survive the perfect storm of a split.

So get to it.

Chapter 6
The First Few Minutes

Okay, I told you that even if you were not at all prepared ahead of time, that I was bringing you some help anyway. So, let's get to that here and over these next few chapters.

When our split happened, it was at the worst possible moment; the end of Sunday morning worship, with a packed house and plenty of visitors. And it was not a quiet affair; with no warning, people started getting up and shouting and making accusations. And then, apparently at a given signal, the main ringleader and another confidant (who, suspiciously, were sitting directly across the aisle from each other in seats that they had never sat in before) got up and stormed out, and a substantial number of people got up and followed them out.

I have used the word before, but I will use it here again now; I was blindsided. And it is nothing but the pure grace of God preserving me that allowed me to do exactly what needed to be done in the next few minutes because, as with a heart attack or stroke, the first few minutes are crucial.

Everything in my flesh wanted to scream at them from the pulpit as they left, call them liars, and tell them to never come back. But much of the congregation was sitting there with their jaws hanging open, others with tears streaming down their faces, and everyone was clearly scared.

So, pushing the desires of my flesh aside, I spoke calmly to the congregation, and my words went something like this. "Ladies and gentlemen, I am not sure what all is going on, but we are not angry with those who just left or with anyone else. But we are also not going to let any of this stop us from faithfully doing what we are still supposed to be doing as God's people. So, let's close in prayer, and I will see you all back here tonight for evening worship."

The effect was what I hoped for. People calmed down, and then I closed in prayer (normally, I would have had another gentleman do that, but as you may have guessed by now, my "closer" had just left as well, sigh...), a very loooooong prayer, a prayer that was heavy on praising God, and silent on what had just transpired. Instinctively, I knew that my people needed to hear me talking confidently to God; they needed to know that He was still there and that I was still His man, and that things would somehow be okay. And then, once the prayer was done, I rushed to the doors to greet everyone on their way out. I shook hands, I hugged the itty-bitty children as always, I laughed and smiled – and all the while, I was dying inside. But I knew, I just knew that I could not let any of that show. I knew we were balanced on the edge of a razor and that any wrong move would be fatal.

Pastor, I pray that you never have a split. But if you do, I hope that you remember this chapter, and I hope you make the first few crucial moments count. Do not lash out, do not shout, do not threaten, do not cry. You have been God's man for the church up until that moment. You have been the one others looked to for strength and stability. So, even while you are reeling on the inside like a man who has just insulted Mike Tyson while crammed into a phone booth with him, stand, smile, be sweet, be firm, and be confident on the outside.

Make the first few moments count; your very survival depends on it.

Chapter 8
The Next Service

The entire church split thing was still absolutely brand new to me, so I was very much flying by the seat of my pants. You have no idea how often I look back and say, "Lord, thank you for putting clear thoughts in my head when my own thoughts were JAUBMLDEMSES" (Let me know when you figure that one out!)

Among the clear thoughts that God gave me pretty quickly was that the very next service, Sunday evening, would be terribly important. For people on the fence to show up for church and see thirty or forty percent of the normally filled seats empty would be horrific. But what was I to do?

A situation like this is where good friends are really valuable.

A township over, a pastor friend of mine held his evening services at five in the afternoon, while ours back in the day were at seven. So I called him, explained the situation, and said, "Is there any way at all that you can bring some of your folks over with you to our service once you are done with yours?"

And he did. We had a really big crowd that night!

Now, clearly (especially since I openly thanked them for coming out to our services and called their pastor and church by name), no one was "fooled" into thinking that any of the folks from that church intended to become members of our church. That was never the point. The point was to avoid having shaky people show up at the service after a split and see a bunch of empty seats. And on that solely relevant criteria, the plan was an absolute success. Our people instinctively fell into their normal hospitable behavior, greeting everyone, making sure they all got good seats, and even doing the standard Christian hobby of finding out how they may possibly be related, if they ever worked together, etcetera.

I let many of their special singers do the singing that night since (in another non-surprise) we also lost most of our special singers in the split. And from my post on the platform, I could see God ministering peace and comfort to the hearts of my scared people through those dear folks who went to their own church and then came to mine to throw us a lifeline when we needed it the most.

Elizabeth, my genius wife, ran the sound booth that night (did I mention that we also lost our sound booth crew in the split? I probably should have mentioned that) and, as with everything she does, did so seemingly effortlessly.

We came through the first post-split service with flying colors.

Pastor, your first post-split service is pretty important. So, even though your heart is going to be aching and your head is going to be spinning, I need you to do something. Slow down... take several deep breaths... and think. What gaps will need to be filled by the very next service? Who can you quickly put in place so that things move along as if not a single person has left? And what can you do to fill up some empty pews? Send out an SOS to friends, family, other pastors, and do your very best to minimize the empty spots in the next service. Offer to treat people to a meal afterward, if necessary; this is an acceptable use of those emergency funds!

During that service, I did not mention what had happened that morning; I literally behaved as if nothing out of the ordinary had happened at all! It was many years later before I learned that the ring leaders still had "plants" among us reporting on all that went on in the post-split days and weeks and that they were really blown away that we seemed to not even remember it by that evening!

You can do it, Pastor; smile and worship God and project joy in that first service after the split.

Chapter 7
The Next Couple of Hours

Once we left church on that fateful Sunday morning, we went to a quick lunch, then went to battle. There were several families who had not been there that morning due to sickness or travel, and I wanted to get to them before our adversaries did. I knew this was going to be a race against time.

So, I started lighting up the phones. Sitting at lunch while consoling our shell-shocked children, we also made a list. Having access to all of the church records is pretty handy at a time like that. I called every single family that had been absent, and I told them everything that had happened.

Mind you, I was careful not to say harsh things about those who had shouted/stormed out. I knew that everyone I was talking to would be hearing from them shortly if they had not done so already. And this let me know that it would be a contest of credibility, and I wanted to come across as the level-headed, credible source while others did all of the accusing and shrieking.

How did that go? Pretty well, actually. Roughly two-thirds of the families I called heard from me first, and the other one-third were more than willing to hear my side of the story. And we kept the vast majority of them. In fact, some of them were already aware the split was going to happen and apologetic that they had said nothing, and my forgiving them was all the impetus they needed to stay with us.

We also, while calling others, got a few very angry phone calls on the incoming side. All of them were from the main leaders of the split and their immediate family members. And in each case, all of them wanted to have a screaming match on the phone. Also, in each case, when the screaming started, I told each one, "I will be praying for you, goodbye," then hung up and made the next call to someone else. I knew that their minds were absolutely irrevocably made up, so they were not my goal. They were not even my members anymore, as all of them made very clear by shrieking something like, "We are never coming back!" So, why would I waste time with them when others could likely be salvaged?

And, by not lashing out at any of them, I took away any potential ammunition of that type that many of them would no doubt have loved me to hand them.

Your first few hours after a split will be a whirlwind of calls and now of texts, chats, posts, and a bunch of other newfangled things that I did not need to worry about back then. Be very careful to use those first few hours wisely; spend them shoring up support from those on the fence.

Let the wolves howl; you have sheep to protect.

Chapter 9
The Hardest Week

Monday mornings have a reputation amongst pastors. Monday is the day when every pastor resigns over and over again before trying again the following Sunday!

But believe me when I tell you, the Monday after a split, and the entire week after a split, really, is brutally hard. Aside from the midweek prayer service (I know some churches do not have those anymore; ours did and does), Monday through Saturday is a dangerous post-split time, a time when you do not have the power of the pulpit to help you calm and encourage your people. It is the week when the phone lines are melting down, and those who want to see you destroyed are very active in calling everyone and cajoling them to leave, promising that things will be much better in the new church they plan to start.

But do you know what superpower you have, especially if you are a full-time pastor? You have lots of hours to hop in your vehicle and go knock on the doors of your church families.

And we did.

All week long, we went family to family, sitting down in living rooms and letting people variously tell us they loved us, or tell us they were angry with us, or tell us they had concerns. And we did way more listening than talking; that is pretty important.

We did not spend any time trying to discredit those who were trying to discredit us. Instead, we spent our time trying to shore up connections at the heart level with people that we dearly loved. We bit our tongues a lot; many things were said that were really hurtful. I will particularly never forget having a person we had helped a great deal through the years shout, "How could you possibly be so stupid?" over my perceived flaws in all of the messy ordeal. My calm answer (that did not match what was raging in my heart) was, "I can indeed be very stupid, I suppose. But I am more than willing to learn. So, what do you think I need to learn to handle things better next time?"

That individual is still with us all of these long years later and is one of our staunchest allies and advocates.

We also spent some time that week doing the exact same thing we had always done through the years, knocking on doors to tell people about Jesus and about the church. All we really wanted to do was stay home in the dark each day and cry, but we did not. We cried in the car a lot instead...

And the funny thing about visiting when you do not feel like it is that God very much seems to honor it more than ever. We had visitors the very next Sunday who are still with us to this day.

It was a long and painful week. But handling it as we did (again, all by the grace of God since I had no clue at all what I was doing) helped us to survive that first week and laid the groundwork for a much brighter future.

Chapter 10
Incoming! (And What to Do About It)

A couple of weeks after the split, we found ourselves dealing with a new and unforeseen problem, namely the mail!

"Pastor, um, I thought you should know that this came yesterday," one of my men said sheepishly as he met me in the foyer. He was holding a letter in his hand – and so were the next several people behind him! As it turns out, one of the principal figures in the split had decided to write everyone a duplicate letter explaining why he and the rest of the splitters were right and how wrong I was about everything.

Let me say, right off the bat, kudos to every member with the character to come straight to their pastor with a letter like that. That situation let me know how much confidence I could safely have in people!

I took the letter(s) into the office and sat down with them and picked one to read. It was all of the same old same old that had already been hurled at us, complete with a few more choice accusations. And every single remaining family in our church had received one.

Every. One.

As I will make clear in a later chapter, there are things that you will be wise to simply ignore altogether. But when (and in the days of social media, it is probably going to be a when, not an if) one of those who wants to destroy you has made direct contact with your remaining sheep in an effort to draw them away from the fold, you actually do need to deal with that.

The only question is how.

The short answer is "tactfully."

The longer version of that answer is, "You still have the church, and you are still standing, so handle this type of thing as the generous victor, not as a floundering and desperate loser flailing about trying to stay alive."

A few moments after reading the letter and after having prayed fast and fervently over it, I headed into the pulpit to begin the service. And I did not mention the letter at all – yet.

We proceeded with the service as normal, and I made sure that every song was a bright and cheery one and that every announcement sounded like the Ice Cream Truck was pulling into the parking lot. I actually even changed my message at the last minute to one that was more encouraging than what I had originally planned.

Feel free to accuse me of being opportunistic if you like; I prefer to think of it as trying to stave off a church collapse for one more day.

Once the service was done, I asked the members if they could stick around for a few minutes, and then I closed in prayer and dismissed the visitors. Once they were gone, I smiled at everyone, the biggest smile I could come up with, held up one of the letters, laughed a bit, and said, "So, how many of you have gotten one of these?"

All hands went up.

At this point, you likely think that I went through it point by point to refute it all.

Nope.

"So, since you have all read this, and since most of it is all of the same old stuff, then you already know it isn't true, so there is no use in me rehashing any of that. But," I said, "there are a couple of new things, so let's quickly get those out of the way, too."

Then, I very quickly and calmly pointed out the new things and dismantled them in a very measured tone of voice.

All of it took less than two minutes.

Then I said, "Now, Sam is hurting, and he is lashing out. So, what should Christians do when other people are hurting?"

"Um, I guess we should pray for them?" came a timid answer from a man in the congregation.

"That is the correct answer," I said. "So, let's do that right now."

Then I led the church in prayer for Sam and his entire family. I prayed for their repentance and restoration, I prayed for their children not to stray from the Lord through all of this, I prayed for his mother's failing health, and I prayed for him to be safe in the dangerous job he worked.

I prayed for two or three times as long as I dealt with the letter. Then I said, "Amen," the congregation echoed it, and I completely let the matter drop.

And so did everyone else.

And that, Pastor, is the entire point and is way better than getting into another mortar lobbing contest.

Diffuse rather than detonate.

Chapter 11
You Still Have to Preach (And Here Is How)

Under the very best of circumstances, preaching is still a very difficult endeavor. It requires long, patient hours of studying words, phrases, backgrounds, and context. It requires an extreme mental effort to decide what needs to be put in, what needs to be left out, how to arrange it all, and a thousand other considerations.

But the hardest part of all, bar none, is simply knowing *what* to preach each service. The Bible is a very big book, after all, and the possibilities are boundless!

But after a split, one realizes in horror that all of this must still be done, even while you feel as if you have been completely gutted and could die at any moment. I cannot begin to adequately describe to you how agonizing a task it was to prepare to preach and then to preach, especially in the first several months after the split. As I look back now at my list of messages, there are not many messages from those days that I would ever want to re-preach. All of them still seem very hollow to me to this day.

It got bad. It got so bad, in fact, that I am convinced I would not have survived save for one thing. In desperation at having to pray and think over what to preach each week when it seemed like my prayers were not getting past the ceiling, I changed my prayer from "Lord, what do you want me to preach this Sunday?" to "Lord, what do you want me to preach for the next few years?" Somehow, I knew that if I could just get an answer to that one prayer, the hardest part of sermon preparation would be taken off of the table for an extended period of time, a period of time that I was just trying to survive.

And God, in mercy, answered my prayer. I was to preach through the gospels! On Sunday mornings, I would still do a topical message, but on evening services, I would go verse-by-verse through those life-giving books.

I was thinking in terms of a few years; God was thinking in terms of the next decade.

For a decade or more, there was not a question of what Sunday nights and Wednesday nights would hold. Whatever passage came next was it. And as a bonus, I would not be "tailor making" any fire and brimstone messages designed to hit my adversaries square in the eye from a distance.

Pastor, the stress of a split can kill a man. Add to that the stress of trying to figure out what to preach and then trying to actually do it, and you have a recipe for ruin. So, my advice to you is pray, ask God to give you a book or section of Scripture to preach through, and then bask in the wonder of the Word as its words wash away your hurts one passage at a time.

Chapter 12
The "Keys" To Success

Throwing down the keys on the way out the door is somewhat of a staple in church splits. Unfortunately, I also learned the hard way that there is a much worse thing that sometimes happens, namely that people either do not turn in the keys or that they have made copies that you did not know about! And that and related issues, Pastor, are things that you need to be aware of so that you can head trouble off at the pass.

These days, most every church (including mine) has an extensive camera system that allows one to play back weeks worth of footage. But back in the days of our perfect storm, we did not yet have that in place. We had an alarm, mind you, but the same people that had keys to the building also had codes to the alarm!

For weeks, we kept coming into the church to find that things seemed to have been "messed with." We were already a jumbled bundle of nerves and definitely did not need that happening as well! But when I came in one day to find an accusatory note pinned on a bulletin board, I knew good and well that none of our still remaining people were to blame. And that left only those who were gone – many of whom had been given keys through the years.

It was expensive, but the very next week, all of the locks were changed, and all of the alarm codes were reset. Not surprisingly, from that point on, nothing got messed with, and no notes were left for us.

But that small thing led me to examine even bigger issues of access. For one thing, one of our trustees had left during the split as well (Did I not mention that? I really should have mentioned that…), and he still had access to certain church accounts!

Pretty quickly, therefore, we called a church business meeting and reset our trustees as well. Then we went to the bank the very next day and had all access limited to just the handful of current people that needed it.

Pastor, if you have gone through a split, you are likely in survival mode and thinking only of the people in the pews and the very next service. But you are going to need to think in broader terms if you are going to survive, and that is going to include things like changing locks and removing access to those who no longer need it.

Chapter 13
"Ah Ah Ah Ah Stayin'
Aliiiiiiiiiiiiiiiiive!"

Please allow me to thoroughly impress you with another demonstration of my mental prowess:

Dead people don't win wars.

I know, I know, you are in awe of my great understanding of military matters; you may feel free to call me "General Rivers" if you like.

Seriously, though, dead people actually do not win wars!

A few months after our split, when the aftershocks just kept coming one right after the other, I found myself lying on the floor of my office clutching my chest, feeling it get tighter and tighter. I was seriously contemplating shouting for my secretary to dial 911, but finally, by slowing my breathing dramatically and lying very still, the pressure eased up.

By the way, if you ever feel that way, do NOT point back to this chapter and refuse to dial

911. Go ahead and do so; better to be safe than, well, dead.

Anyway, later that night, I got home, headed into the restroom to take a shower, took my shirt off – then absolutely gasped when I looked in the mirror. Who was this chap with the belly hanging over his trousers? And why had I not noticed this "issue" before?

"Because you have been too busy winning the world to whittle your waist," I said, pleased with my impromptu alliteration but disgusted with my protruding paunch. And I knew that if something did not change, the combination of my belly and my battle was going to kill me. And at that moment, I made a choice:

"I am going to outlive every last one of those knuckleheads."

Yes, I know, that is not exactly Spurgeonesque. But I meant it.

The next day, I had a gym membership, a new scale, and lots of fruit, vegetables, and lean protein in the house. Junk food? Gone. Soft drinks and table salt? Forbidden. And I went at it with a passion; in four months, I lost the entire "paunch" and replaced it with a respectable set of abs. My breathing was easier, my headaches were gone, and my chest did not hurt anymore despite all of the attacks that continued to beset us. And I have maintained that healthy lifestyle and slimmed-down physique through all of these years.

I found something out; I not only like living, I like all of the things that make it more likely for me to continue to do so!

Pastor, your "profession," if it can be so called, is uniquely designed to kill you. You sit around a lot, eat tons of unhealthy food, and deal with stress that the average factory worker will never fully fathom. And when you add a church split on top of that, it may well be enough to make you assume room temperature, also known in less colloquial terms as "dying."

And dead people don't win wars, especially when that war is a church split.

So take a look in the mirror. If your first reaction is something akin to horror or denial, and if your scale flashes a "One at a time, please" message up to you, it is time to radically change your lifestyle.

If you want to survive your perfect storm, you have to actually stay alive.

Chapter 14
Family Matters

Pastor, I cannot emphasize what I am about to say strongly enough; if your family does not survive the split, the devil has won, no matter what happens with your church.

I have already told you that when our storm hit, our children were devastated. Obviously, Elizabeth and I were as well, but the fact that our children were crying themselves to sleep each night was way harder to deal with than us crying ourselves to sleep.

As the weeks dragged on and more and more people left, I could see my children spiraling into a depression. I also knew that many pastor's children have been ruined forever by seeing things go badly in church. And Elizabeth and I were determined not to let that happen.

By this time, we were in all-out survival mode. I actually took a reduction in salary from the church and supplemented that loss by doing side jobs during the week just to give the church a longer cash burn runway, as well as selling a vehicle that I really liked and getting something much cheaper in its place. But I knew that finances were the least of my worries; my children were dying on the inside.

But children were not the only consideration.

For her part, Elizabeth took a lot of hits all during the split and the aftermath. She was the subject of just as many accusations, just as many innuendos, and just as many outright lies. To top that off, certain people made sure that she also heard horrible things, not just about me, but even about our children, and that nearly sent her over the edge. And it was when she threatened to *ahem* cut off certain parts of a man's anatomy and hand them back to him that I knew I needed to help her get some healing as well.

A few days off is significantly cheaper than a defense attorney.

For us, each day started with us driving the children to school, a very good Christian school one county over. We used that time to do our family morning devotions as well, reading a Bible passage to them, then praying, then reading a chapter or two from some Christian book such as something from The Chronicles of Narnia. And then, once all of that was done, things would be silent on the last few minutes before we got to school with them.

On this day, though, we turned down different roads and just kept on going without saying a word. Finally, Winston looked up and realized we were in unfamiliar territory.

"Where are we?" he asked.

"Oh, just somewhere we have never been before," I replied mysteriously.

Instantly, we had their full attention and were getting peppered with questions. So, we turned it into a guessing game. After half an hour, they finally learned that we were on the way to the newly opened aquarium near their grandparents' home, two states away. We had arranged for them to be out of school for the week, and we used that time for a family adventure. And for two days, children who had had nothing on their minds except for their hurts and lost friends thought only of sting rays, sharks, and all things under the sea.

They saw fascinating creatures; their mother and I saw relief and healing washing over them. And while Elizabeth was watching them heal, I could see her healing as well; knowing that her children and husband would be okay was better than any stress medication anyone could have ever offered her.

We started taking the children hiking pretty regularly. We had family board game nights. And (their personal favorite), we started doing a weekly pizza and movie night. And by this time, new families were joining, families with children about their ages, so we started arranging play dates with these new children and their parents. Those new children quickly became my children's very best friends; they are still in church with us to this day, and they are all still ultra-close.

We also were very careful not to speak of the split in front of our children unless they themselves brought it up and wanted to talk about it. And we never, ever spoke ill of church or the ministry; there is nothing more fatal that a pastor can ever do than to teach his children that the ministry is some horrible hardship.

Elizabeth and I bit our tongues for a very long time around our children. It was really only when they became young adults that we told them most everything, and then only in the context of how good God had been to us the entire way.

I made sure that Elizabeth and I had a date night pretty regularly. Mind you, Pastor, this ought to be standard operating procedure for you and your bride anyway! But especially when everything inside you just wants to shut down, you need to be sure to keep dating your mate. Far too many pastor's homes have split up and failed due to the stress of a church split.

When you are facing your split, then, you need to be very watchful of your wife and children. Never let them be under the pressure for too long. Go new places, have new adventures, see new things. And guard your marriage; the devil would love to have that above all.

Chapter 15

The Power of "The Next Thing"

Okay, Pastor, if I told you that you have in your possession a magic wand that could wave a lot of troubles away, *Poof!* would you use it?

Don't be pious; you know you would.

And you do. And for a small love offering of just $99.95...

I am kidding about that offering; you already bought the book, and the instructions to the wand come with it.

The wand I am talking about is "The Next Thing." The Next Thing has a power that you cannot possibly imagine. And God was so gracious to help me instinctively know this when trying to survive our perfect storm. For a few weeks, people came into church sheepishly, looking around from side to side. And I knew what they were looking for; they were looking to see who would be missing that week, never to return. They were looking to see which friends they no longer had. And I knew that if I could not get them looking for something other than that, we would eventually fold like a house of cards.

Enter "The Next Thing."

When a church goes through a split, they usually do the worst thing possible: nothing. They just come to church week after week and watch the congregation get smaller, the choir get quieter, the offerings get tinier, and morale get lower.

I knew we would not survive that.

A couple of weeks after the split, I stood in the pulpit and did the last thing anyone was expecting: I announced two different special speakers who would be with us in the next few weeks.

And then, after that, I announced a brand new Christmas series.

And then we had a brand new Christmas play.

And then, I announced a soup cook-off for the cold days of January, complete with judges and trophies, and also told them that one of our sister churches would be participating.

And then, after that, I announced a Spring Bible Conference that I was so excited about!

People were not sure what to make of it; we had always been an active church, but now we were a whirlwind of activity.

And there was a method to the madness. By keeping everyone worshipping and laughing and fellowshipping and eating together and doing fun activities, people stopped looking around at empty seats and started enjoying church again.

But the big one was still coming, and to this day, even to me, it seems utterly insane. But I had prayed about it for long months and was very sure that God wanted it to be our next "The Next Thing."

"Ladies and gentlemen," I said as I stood before them on a bright Sunday morning, "Don't you all think it's about time for us to have a Family Life Center?"

I need you to understand this; even I was not sure from week to week if we would survive financially. And here I was, bringing up the least likely thing imaginable: the idea of building another building.

I still remember the various looks on people's faces. Some of the old-timers had a "Yep, he's finally cracked under the pressure" look. Newer members, largely oblivious to what had happened before they arrived, looked very excited. A few who were really tuned in to everything looked like, "Absolutely, let's go to battle; we will show them that we don't intend to quit!"

And a year or so later, we broke ground. Once again, this would take everyone helping somehow. And that, everyone digging and cleaning and framing and serving meals and so many other facets of construction together so occupied everyone's attention that, for the couple of years the project went on, there was little to no mention of the storm at all.

And, in case you wonder how big God really is, we had it paid for in full by the time the project was done.

Mind you, I am not saying that starting a building project will solve your split problems. If you think that, please put this book down and walk away from it! I am merely emphasizing again the power of "The Next Thing." I am not exaggerating when I tell you that I did not let so much as a week go by without some kind of next thing either going on or being planned for.

We took church trips to Amish country and to St. Augustine and to Washington, D.C. We did day trips to farmer's markets. We announced special nights to eat out together, "whosoever will may come" type of gatherings. It was my specific intention to keep everyone way too busy to think about the split or to spend any time with the splitters! In my mind, it was a metaphorical turbo-charged church bus with the pedal to the medal carrying us away from the trouble at top speed.

There were many times that Elizabeth, knowing how exhausted I was, would say, "You really need to slow down," and I would answer, "Not quite yet; we still haven't put enough distance between us and the storm."

Pastor, I know you are hurting. Lots of others are as well, though. And for their sake, you need to wave the wand.

Do not neglect the awesome power of The Next Thing.

Chapter 16

The Danger of Greener Pastures

It occurs to me that I have not yet really told you how long it took for us to "get over" our split.

Brace yourself; you might not like the answer.

Ten years.

Now, please do not misunderstand me. We actually started the healing process pretty quickly, and there was seemingly not a week that went by that we did not have some new blessing from God for which to be grateful. But what every pastor in a split situation really wants to know is basically how long it will take them to be fully recovered, and by fully recovered, they are generally thinking in terms of things like membership, attendance, finances, and the ability to go for a long period of time without even thinking of the storm.

I suppose for some churches, all of that comes pretty quickly. For us, as I noted above, it was about ten years. And I mention that now in order to warn you of a particularly subtle danger, a trap that the devil will no doubt lay for you, the lovely lure of greener pastures.

A few short years after our storm, we were still under just as much pressure as we had ever been. The devil had, in fact, still been piling things onto us week after week after week, determined to destroy us while we were down.

And in the midst of all of that pressure, I walked out of my office and into the auditorium just before service on a lovely Sunday morning to see several suit-wearing, dignified-looking men sitting together on the back row, none of whom I had ever seen before.

In case you do not know, that is what a pulpit committee generally looks like.

I saw all of our people greeting them cordially, as they always do, and I shook my head slowly as a thin smile crossed my face. "They are here for your pastor, and you don't even know it," I mumbled to myself.

Sure enough, after service, they asked to speak to me in the office. And it did not take them long at all to get down to business. As it turns out, they were from a large church in a decent-sized city, a church whose pastor had just resigned.

And they wanted me to candidate to be the new pastor.

Due to my crazy schedule (mostly all of those "The Next Things" I just told you about), it was going to be a few months before I could get there.

But those few months passed faster than I could have imagined. And thus it was that Elizabeth and I and our children found ourselves pulling into a massive parking lot at the end of which was a massive building that stood in the shadow of a large city and all of its tall buildings. We parked, walked inside, and I heard Winston say, "Whoaaaaa!" That was his way of expressing his amazement at how big everything was. My wife and daughters were quiet, but their eyes were all wide.

We were greeted cordially by the staff and ushered into the office to meet the interim pastor. And a few moments later, we were taken into the auditorium where I saw what I, to this day, still affectionately call "the Jumbotrons," mounted on either side behind the pulpit.

As I preached that day, both morning and evening, I had myself over each shoulder; that is a really weird feeling if you have never experienced it!

The building was large; the crowd was large; the noise was large. For a small-town pastor, this was a dream come true, waiting to happen.

The entire family was excited as we drove home the next day. For her part, Elizabeth was already looking up potential houses!

As the glow of that glorious day faded, though, a harsh reality set in for me. By leaving for these greener pastures, I would gain a huge salary, a huge congregation to preach to, and a huge house to live in. But doing so would effectively make sure that I never regained the one thing that I had lost that meant the most to me:

My reputation.

Many years ago, Solomon wrote these words, "*A good name is rather to be chosen than great riches, and loving favour rather than silver and gold.*" (Proverbs 22:1)

For many years, I had built up a good reputation, a good name in our community. And all of that had been snatched away in one angry moment of time. And I knew that if I left for those greener pastures, those who still wished to see us destroyed would flood the community with, "See?!? This is exactly what we have been telling you. He is a charlatan; he is just in it for the money!"

Calling those dear people from that large church and telling them that we could not come is, to this day, one of the very hardest things I have ever done. But, as it turns out, it ultimately became one of the most valuable things I have ever done. As the years went on and we stayed faithful, I earned back my reputation in the community to such a degree that even many of those who left in the split openly tell others how honest and honorable they view me to be.

I am not telling you that there is never a time to leave after a split. The reason I am not telling you that is because you are God's servant, not mine, and He can bid people leave or stay at His pleasure.

But I am telling you, unequivocally, that the vast majority of the time, leaving after a split makes things worse in the long run, not better. Normally, you leave your reputation at the mercy of the wolves who tried to devour you and then find that things are no better in your "greener pastures."

Please allow me to encourage you a bit, here. It has been many years since our split. And, having stuck it out, here are some of the things we have been able to enjoy.

One particular gentleman who swore that he would never set foot on the property again ended up moving away to another state. And yet, each time he comes back to our area for a visit, he comes to our church, and it is just like he never left. He even comes on many of our special trips with us!

Another family eventually came back and apologized and rejoined the church, and they were here until work moved them to another state.

Other families have sent notes apologizing for their part in the storm.

Our church is now the biggest church in town and has an open door to minister to the entire community at public events.

I could go on at length in this. Just trust me when I tell you that leaving for greener pastures may be a quick fix to surface problems, but staying and weathering the storm and its aftermath is a long-term fix to far deeper problems.

Chapter 17
Keep It Out of the Pulpit (and Offline!)

When you have been through a split, second only to the temptation to punch people in the mouth is the temptation to relitigate the split in the pulpit service after service after service. Trust me; this is a temptation that I fought every single week for at least two years. After all, the power of the pulpit is an awesome thing! How wonderful would it be to have a captive audience listening to you as you rip your enemies to shreds?

And that, Pastor, is exactly what the devil wants.

For starters, every service that you waste preaching about split or splitters is a service that you neglect either the gospel or Biblical doctrine, or both.

Secondly, even if you are absolutely in the right and accurate in everything that you say, you are ripping open everyone's wounds every time you say it.

"But I want people to know my side!"

Listen to me carefully. If it is truly necessary for you to explain your side, then as soon as possible after the split, dismiss all of the visitors, turn off all of the cameras, calmly and kindly explain everything, take and answer questions, dismiss the meeting, and then, this is key:

Shut up.

I have almost lost count of the number of preachers who complain that they never can seem to get their church over the split, the very split that they keep on talking about!

Think about it: you have an army of enemies out there who would love to be able to stand in your pulpit and keep the storm raging on, but who cannot do so, and then you hop up there and do it for them!

To paraphrase an old quote often attributed to John Wayne, "Ministry is hard; it's harder when you're stupid."

A lot of social media was sort of new when we went through our split, and we did not do much on it. These days, though, pastors need to be warned that not only should they keep the split out of the pulpit, they should also keep it off of their social media sites. You do realize, don't you, that if people have tried to destroy you, they are going to do their best to check in to see how successful they are being? They are going to stalk your profiles and watch your live broadcasts and see if they can see you bleed.

So, when they do, let them see... Cat memes. And pictures of your piping hot cups of tea. And political rants. And birthday pictures. And messages where you glorify Jesus and tell everyone how wonderful Christian life is.

In the criminal justice world, alleged perpetrators are read their Miranda rights, among which are the words "Anything you say can be used against you." After a split, you should have those words ringing through your mind pretty regularly!

If you go into the pulpit and complain about how hard things are, it will be used against you.

If you go online and vent about how angry you are, it will be used against you.

If you pound the pulpit and demand that everyone ostracize everyone who left, believe me, that will most definitely be used against you!

Yes, I know that if people had any sense, they would break ties with people who hate their church and their pastor without having to be told to do so. But generally, people do not think of things like that. And if you thunder about it from the pulpit, you are going to come across as the bad guy at the exact time that the splitters are out there calling you... the bad guy.

So, in the words of what seems to be the Colonies' favorite phrase of encouragement, suck it up, buttercup. Use the pulpit to preach the gospel and to teach doctrine and to encourage those who are hurting and to glorify Christ. Use your social media to paint the world a picture of how wonderful it is to be a Christian.

Rubbish is for the dump, not for the pulpit, and not for your social media.

Chapter 18
Split? What Split?

Dovetailing off of the truth of the previous chapter, please allow me to take the subject a bit further in this one. In the years following our split, I became much more aware of other churches and other splits and other pastors, and especially how those other pastors dealt with their splits. In one rather memorable instance, I sat in a meeting with scores of preachers and hundreds of people and listened to a rotund reverend loudly make this boast from the pulpit, "We have had seven splits so far, and I expect that we will have more, and I don't give a rip!"

At that moment, I had a difficult time ascertaining which was more ridiculous to me, his appearance or his asininity. He looked like a 500-pound ball of lard, and it seemed that, at any moment, his gigantic bald red head might explode.

Finally, though, I determined that his asininity was indeed even more ridiculous than his appearance. For starters, anyone who enjoys a church split as much as he apparently does was apparently dropped on his head as a child.

From the top of the Empire State Building.

Secondly, though, and more importantly to our discussion, any pastor who continually brings up the splits of the past is advertising that they have had a split/splits! And I cannot think of a worse way to dissuade new potential members from joining and taking the place of those who have been lost.

May I tell you something that is, perhaps, a bit surprising? I have not spoken of our split save to family and a few close friends since a month or two after it happened. And the result has been that the vast majority of my current church literally does not know that we ever had a split! They will certainly find out now, seeing as how I am writing a book, but I think that will be okay at this point since so many long years have passed.

Our church has a huge group of absolutely wonderful people. Some of them, though, are a bit timid by nature, and I have no problem with that whatsoever. But if, when they started coming to our church, they had heard that we had been through a brutal split, I can absolutely assure you that they would never have visited for a second time. I can also assure you that many of the good people that we had then and still have now would have eventually left if we had continued to talk about it. Most people want to live peaceful lives, and whether you are the one causing the trouble or not, they shy away from things that are constantly stirred up.

So, if you want to survive your perfect storm, you might want to consider taking this very practical step:

Stop talking about it.

Chapter 19
Random Meetings

If you are truly spiritual, then when you wake up in the morning and are, unbeknownst to you, going to run into one of the "other side" of your split that day, God will reveal it to you in a vision to prepare you for it...

No. He won't.

And no, you almost certainly will not be expecting it in the least.

And these are the moments that, if you are not philosophically and emotionally and spiritually prepared for, can end up causing you a lot of harm. Trust me; the devil knows how to put someone on the same garden gnome aisle at The Home Depot that you are on at the very moment you are reaching for the one holding the tiny sign that says "Too Blessed To Be Stressed!"

After our split, it seemed that it was the devil's great joy to bring people along at restaurants, or stores, or funerals, the latter of which I suppose I should have seen coming. Thankfully, God seemingly always allowed us to have a smile, and a level head, and the right words. But there were multiple occasions where I came within a split second of saying or doing the wrong thing – a mistake that could have further ruined the reputation we were trying to rebuild and/or give credence to the attacks that were being leveled against us. Worse still, had Elizabeth or I responded wrongly, it would most assuredly have been used to re-stir the stink that was beginning to settle down!

So please allow me to give you a few words of advice on that, things to (like Daniel) purpose in your heart before it ever comes down to it.

To begin with, purpose in your heart from day one that when accusations or snide comments are slung your way (as is usually the case with the first few random meetings), you will put your anger in the fuel tank, not in the cannon. By that, I mean you are going to get angry over it unless you are some super spiritual psychopath who dreams in King James English and has only "Crown Him With Many Crowns" playing in your head all day as a mental soundtrack. Anger, though, while it often cannot be avoided (especially when blindsided), can be channeled rather than chambered. It can be used as fuel rather than as firepower.

On multiple occasions in the first couple of years after our storm, we ended up getting surprised by these random meetings, and almost invariably, some hateful, snide comment was made. In each case, the next few days became some of the most productive days of my entire ministry! Construction projects magically got done, and bunches of doors were knocked on, and I got way ahead on my exegesis for sermon series, and even projects at home that had been languishing were suddenly finished. Looking back, I sometimes teasingly wonder whether my dear wife was arranging some of these meetings just so her bathroom renovation would finally get done!

Seeing attacks turn into progress made me, as crazy as it may sound, truly thankful for them. I know that God used them for our good, helping us to move forward faster than we had been moving!

Another thing to decide well before any random meetings catch you by surprise is that you will have been genuinely praying for people and that you will, therefore, have some questions to ask, and therefore a good way to manage what will doubtless be an awkward conversation. You see, you know these people, and there was a time when you were their shepherd. Because of that, you prayed for their lost loved ones and wayward children; you prayed for their health needs; you prayed for all kinds of things for them.

And this makes it possible when a splitter suddenly accosts you in public with, "Soooo, how's the church going, huh?" for you to say,

"Going very well. How is your mom's heart? We have been praying that the medicine would be working" or something of that nature. And if that approach sounds vaguely familiar, this is probably why:

Proverbs 15:1 *A soft answer turneth away wrath: but grievous words stir up anger.*

Mind you, your flesh probably does not want to turn away wrath. Your flesh probably wants to fold someone's clothes for them while they are still wearing them! But your flesh is a horrible guide on pretty much everything. And, as a pleasant bonus, you handling random meetings that way rather than by blowing up sends a pretty powerful message, namely that you view yourself as the victor in the contest. After all, if they are sarcastic to you, but you are speaking to God for them, which one of you is on God's side after all?

Another thing to decide ahead of time is that you will not spout off details about "church progress" that will seem like you are trying to prove that you are doing okay. This, more than most, is a trap that pastors easily fall into in these situations. I know this because I myself did, and it ended up costing me.

In the few years after our split, I was really anxious to tell everyone who left all of the very good things that were happening, and in great detail. And in many cases, I got that opportunity! And I felt really, really great getting to "humble brag" about the new families that had joined, and I did so by name.

Are you catching on, yet, to how stupid that was? People who have left our church and still want to see us destroyed have now been given the names of new people who have joined...

Yes, they contacted them. And yes, they got some of them out. And yes, it was my stupid fault! My pride made me vulnerable to attack, just like Hezekiah's pride in showing the Babylonians all the treasures of his house led to them later invading the city and taking everything.

Realize, then, that when people who want to see you destroyed ask, "How is it going?" they do not have your best interests at heart. Once I caught on to that, I developed a standard answer for that question, an answer that I refer to as "delight then deflect." My standard answer became, "Going well, God has been good. You folks doing okay?" (You may insert a mental picture of Loki aiming his scepter and firing at the old man in Germany and Captain America landing in front of the blast and deflecting it with his shield...)

People do not try to take what they do not know that you have.

Let me say that again: people do not try to take what they do not know that you have.

Letting people know that people are being saved and baptized and the church is growing is fine and dandy. Giving any specific targets that people can aim for is as dumb as the former practice of dumping sewage into the Thames – our main source of drinking water! So let them fume and let them flounder, but do not let them focus on a target.

Finally, be sure to pack your sense of humor with you each and every day in the event of any unexpected meeting. I have found nothing so powerful as a smile and a ready laugh to let people know that we were still standing and had no intentions of cutting and running.

Chapter 20
Don't Take the Bait

Please allow me to make a statement that is so philosophically profound that I suspect no human mind has ever conceived of it up until now:

When people leave, they are not there anymore.

I know, I know, you are blown away by my mental acuity on this one. But, sarcasm aside, please allow me to explain why this very non-profound statement may well be more profound than you think when applied to surviving a church split.

One of the funny things about a church split is that the people who engage in them actually rob themselves of one of the things they want the most, namely knowledge of and power over what is happening in a church. When they get up and storm out and take people with them, they leave behind the knowledge they had while they were there, knowledge of how things are going week by week, and they leave behind power and influence over what is happening. They are not there to vote anymore; they are not there to disrupt services; they are not there to whip people into a frenzy anymore.

But here is what you need to know. Once they realize that they have left those things behind, once it dawns on them that they cannot stir up trouble from within anymore, they will almost always turn to the next best option, namely, getting you to do it for them!

What's that, you say? Did you just mumble, "No one would be that stupid"? If you did, you have never pastored through a church split. Believe me, a pastor under that level of stress is liable to do any number of stupid things if he is not careful – and I almost did!

Several months after our split, just as it seemed things were finally settling down, I received a letter at the church on a Wednesday afternoon. It was a long list of financial misdeeds that the anonymous accuser (as if I did not know exactly who it was) was tagging me with and demanding that the church be made aware of. As I scanned the letter, I got more and more angry. Not just at the untruths but at the absolutely abysmal math! I am not exaggerating this in the least; in red pen, all over the paper, were the most hideous examples of mathematical errors, and I mean simple (yet HUGE) errors in things like addition and subtraction.

I was not just angry, though; I was also bewildered. The accuser was a pretty successful businessperson. Not exactly godly, as I learned the hard way, but very, very good with money. These errors absolutely had to be intentional. And, knowing this, I stormed toward the auditorium to put it on the pulpit; I made up my mind to blow that stupidity out of the water that very night!

I made it about three steps.

I realize that God does not speak audibly to man these days. But the message He drove home to my heart would not have been any clearer if He did:

"Are you really that gullible?"

Now THAT got my attention.

I stopped dead in my tracks, calmed my emotions, and just listened...

And it did not take me long to hear with my heart and get the message to my head. I was about to do the dumbest thing imaginable. I was about to take the bait. I was about to do what our enemies were no longer present to do themselves! Had I done as I planned to do, had I gone into the pulpit and dissected that accusatory letter, it would have blown the whole thing wide open again just as it was all settling down.

Sheepishly, I replied, "Thank you, Lord. Thank you for protecting me from my own stupidity." Then I turned around, went to my office, filed the letter with the rest of the information from the split, and have not looked at it again in all of the long years since that day. Nor did I ever mention it to anyone other than Elizabeth; you, dear readers, are the first ones other than her to ever be told of it.

I can only imagine what it would be like to go through a split these days with the ubiquitous nature of social media. More times than I can count, I have been made aware of some other church's split on Facebook or Twitter, and almost always from someone who was instrumental in causing it and was clearly looking to stir things back up again from the outside. And far too often, I have seen pastors take the bait, engage in the battle publicly on social media – and lose even more people because of it.

I understand that there are times when critics and criticism must be answered. But, by and large, if you still have enough people and finances to keep going on as usual after a split, then you have won. And a great rule of thumb on that is, "Once you have won, stop playing." If you keep playing long enough, any lead, no matter how large, will eventually disappear!

So don't take the bait.

Chapter 21
Beware of Bitterness

One thing about going through a split is that, at some point, you get to see how you have done through it and how others have done through theirs. Mind you, not as a comparison/competition, but to see what has worked, what hasn't, and what has been downright disastrous. And I can tell you unequivocally that the worst disaster to come out of a split is bitterness; it must be beaten at all costs.

An hour or so from my church, a pastor acquaintance went through a split of his own at about the same time that we did. I like this chap, I really do – but I do not want to be like him. He is faithful, a very good handler of the Word of God, a tremendous soul-winner – and the most bitter human being I have ever seen.

His split was pretty brutal; some very harsh things were said. He ended up with a lot of knives in his back from what should have been friendly hands. Or, another way to put it, his split was pretty much like every other split in the history of churchdom!

He has not gotten over it.

At all.

I was in a meeting at his church, an exceptionally good meeting. The place was packed, the singing was fantastic, the atmosphere was electric, everything was wonderful. And then, while standing in the pulpit with a million-watt smile, his face and attitude changed in the blink of an eye; I am talking about Jekyll/Hyde.

He started blistering everyone and everything, especially those who "don't support the man of God."

I was utterly confused – until someone leaned over to me and said, "Some folks just came in who were involved in a split from here ten years ago."

I would have sworn that whatever happened had happened last week!

That kind of bitterness is exactly what the writer of Hebrews had in mind:

Hebrews 12:15 *Looking diligently lest any man fail of the grace of God; lest any root of bitterness springing up trouble you, and thereby many be defiled;*

That pastor's bitterness has "defiled" many indeed. His wife is still so bitter that her health is failing. Most of his children want nothing to do with church. His membership is declining year by year. Talking to him in person on many different occasions after that meeting, he never fails to bring up the split at some point in the conversation. It is eating him alive from the inside out and poisoning everyone around him.

Pastor, please understand that hurt is one thing, but bitterness is quite another!

A few years after our split, one of the people deeply involved in it became quite ill and needed medical treatment that their insurance company would not pay for. So Elizabeth and I wrote a check and sent it to them to help meet that need. Now, please know that my flesh did not want to do so, at all. But I was periodically battling bitterness myself, and I knew that, based on the pattern of the Good Samaritan, doing for others who have despised you benefits you as much as it does them.

And then, a different family who was instrumental in the split encountered a different disaster, and I got the entire church involved in stretching out to help them. Doing so not only helped my bitterness but taught my church not to be bitter, either!

However you beat it, beat it. Wreck bitterness before it wrecks you and everyone you love.

Chapter 22
The Power of True Forgiveness

Perhaps the most convicting words in Scripture are these that were spoken by Christ.

Matthew 6:14 *For if ye forgive men their trespasses, your heavenly Father will also forgive you:* **15** *But if ye forgive not men their trespasses, neither will your Father forgive your trespasses.*

These words have nothing to do with salvation; we are saved by grace through faith. But they do have everything to do with fellowship and daily blessings. Simply put, if we refuse to forgive others, God will hold it against us in the realm of our fellowship with Him. The relationship is secure; the fellowship is ever-changing based on what we do or do not do.

In the early years after the split, something happened that I predicted would happen. One of the men who left (and by "left" I mean stormed into my office, screamed at me for several minutes, and slammed the door on the way out so hard that I thought it would shatter the frame) was a preacher, a man heading for China to be a missionary.

Fast forward a few years. He was now at another church and on deputation raising his support. And that is when my phone started ringing. You see, a pretty large number of people knew that he had been part of my church and called to ask why he was being sent out of another church. And I told them. I did not do so gleefully, nor did I embellish things in any way. And after a few weeks of this, I received a call from the gentleman. He had clearly not factored in this potentiality!

A couple of days later, he was sitting in my office – the very same office he was last in while screaming and slamming the door. Only this time, he was sheepish and humble. He was also repentant and apologetic, and I mean genuinely so. There was no equivocating; there was no blame shifting; there was just "I completely blew it, and I am sorry."

Now, I knew full well what had precipitated this new meeting. Not being able to raise support is as serious as it gets for a would-be missionary!

So, knowing this, I screamed at the top of my lungs and threw things across the room and scalded him and told him that he had made his bed and could jolly well lie in it...

No, I didn't.

I did not even bring up any of the things I intended to bring up. I actually had a long list I had written down and was staring at, a list of things he needed to answer for, and I simply threw it away. This was a brother who had once served faithfully beside me and had made a terribly bad mistake along the way.

So I forgave him with absolutely no reservations.

And would you like to know the really wonderful part? Some of his family later moved to our town, and they are members of our church now! Better still, while he and I will likely never be part of the same church together again, we now once again talk relatively regularly. And he is doing a good mission work, and I could not be more pleased! What difference will it make in eternity whether he is sent to win the lost out of my church or out of some other good church? The gospel is the gospel either way, and the lost need to hear it.

There was another unique meeting as well, some years after our split. Of all things, I was at Walmart in the grocery aisle. Suddenly, a very familiar voice spoke up behind me, "Hey, Pastor Rivers, how are you?"

I stiffened just a bit. The last time I heard it, the owner of that voice now lived on the other side of the country and was berating me once again by telephone. It was a voice that had, during our storm, stood in a crowd and chewed me up and spit me out.

I turned, and sure enough, it was Tom.

"I'm good," I said a bit cautiously. "How are you?"

He hung his head. "Not so good, really. I did not know if I would run into you while I was in town. I was kind of hoping I wouldn't – but I am glad that I did."

Then he looked up, and I could see the remorse in his eyes.

"I owe you an apology," he said earnestly. "A big one."

He really did; his part in the split and even in all of the damage that happened for the next several months was huge.

"Would you please forgive me?"

This one was tough; without all that he did and said, there never would have been a split to begin with. But if we can only forgive the insignificant things, is it really forgiveness at all?

"I forgive you," I said, and I meant it.

He cried, and we hugged.

We have run into each other three times since that day, and all three meetings have been pleasant.

My blood pressure is good. And, for what it is worth, even now, in my early senior years, I am not on any medication. You see, forgiving is like milk; it does a body good, along with a brain and a psyche. And it also does a family good;

Elizabeth is now once again on very friendly terms with Tom's wife, and my children are again on excellent terms with their children and grandchildren.

But best of all, my fellowship with the Lord has been sweet for years now. I need not preach in the flesh because forgiving has made it possible for me to preach in the power of the Holy Spirit. If you want to survive your split, I suggest you make forgiveness a top priority.

Chapter 23
Renovation and Remodeling After the Storm

Something that I had to get adjusted to when I moved to the States was the incredibly damaging storms that the summer and autumn and even winter often produce. But through the years, I have noticed that human resiliency can often produce some beautiful results. That tornado that came through and wrecked several neighborhoods? Within two years, they were rebuilt and more beautifully than ever. That thunderstorm violent enough to rip shingles off of houses? When the roofs were redone, it was with brightly colored metal instead of the gray shingles that had been scattered abroad. Those flimsy carports that were torn down by the weight of snow and ice? They are now remade in brick or iron and are both stronger and lovelier than ever.

Had any of those neighborhoods either stayed as they were after the storm or even rebuilt exactly like they were before the storm, they likely would have eventually been abandoned entirely. But because people renovated and remodeled after the storm, no one fears to come to those areas.

In the perfect storm of the church split, the damage may not be visible in terms of church buildings or roofs, but believe me, it is very visible to the community around the church that has gone through it. Oftentimes, a church dies during a split and does not know it until years later. By that, I mean when you become known as "that church where all of that stuff happened," if you do not change that perception in the eyes of the community, then those who attempted to destroy you will succeed, even if it takes years for the doors to finally close.

And that is where church renovation and remodeling play such a vital role in surviving the perfect storm.

Please understand that I mean much more than just work on the building and grounds when I say that, though all of that is certainly included. So, starting with the building and grounds, please let me give you some advice, some things that worked well for us – things I trust will work well for you also.

In an earlier chapter, you read of our new Family Life Center. But, as big as that was and is, it does not scratch the surface of all that we did in the months and years after our split. I was determined that 1) when people came in to visit, they would be impressed by what they saw and willing to give us a continued opportunity to woo them, and 2) when people from our past inevitably came to visit for some reason, they would realize that we had continued to move forward with a passion even in their absence. On that one, I took my model from that of Nehemiah rebuilding the walls of Jerusalem and the impact that it had on their enemies:

Nehemiah 6:16 *And it came to pass, that when all our enemies heard thereof, and all the heathen that were about us saw these things, they were much cast down in their own eyes: for they perceived that this work was wrought of our God.*

One of the big divides in Christendom today revolves around the essential doctrine of church pews versus chairs. One simply cannot go to heaven unless their church gets that one right!

Obviously, I am teasing about that. But for many years prior to the split, our church had fallen into the church pew category. A year or so after the split, though, especially since our pews were getting some age on them, having been given to us by another church to begin with, I determined to purchase and install new interlocking chairs for our church. And if you visit us today, you will be sitting on those still lovely chairs that were both for the good comfort of all of our posteriors and for the message-sending value that they possess, namely that we are not what we once were when we endured our storm.

During a funeral a few years after our split, many of the old crowd were in attendance. And the very first words out of the mouth of the main leader of our split, who was in attendance that day, was a half-shocked/half-sarcastic proclamation of, "New chairs!"

Remember, this was the man who proclaimed that he would destroy us financially and see the church shut down! Those chairs served as a cushy reminder that he was failing miserably.

Paint is another wonderful option. In the few short years after the split, we had repainted absolutely every inch of wall in the entire church. Mind you, the walls were not exactly in bad shape; we just wanted as much of a fresh start as we could get and wanted to let our community know that, once again, the past did not define our present.

We re-landscape the entire property. We installed a large and lovely new sign. We re-paved the driveway. We put in a playground for the children. And after all of these years, it is still an ongoing process; a month does not go by that we are not doing something to improve and update the grounds and facilities.

The buildings and grounds are not the only opportunities you have for renovation and remodeling, though.

For several years prior to the split, our church had a radio broadcast on a semi-local station. And, while there was nothing exactly wrong with it, both the name of the broadcast and the theme of the broadcast were, shall we say, somewhat militant. Again, there is nothing wrong with that; Paul told Timothy that we have been called to be soldiers. But when a church has been through a particularly brutal split, trying to woo new members with, "Come on over and get in on all the fighting!" is not exactly a recipe for success.

So we ceased the broadcast for an extended period of time. And then, when we brought it back, it was renamed and had a new theme, something that was much more "peaceful" than "pow pow pow!"

And by that time in history, with social media beginning to be a much bigger player in the church world, we tapped the skills of many of our young people and started putting together a solid and encouraging online presence. I myself ended up with a column in a local periodical, something that I used to encourage people who were hurting and depressed.

Another avenue in which we very successfully renovated and remodeled was in our interactions with the community around us. As we re-grew and as our facilities got bigger and nicer, we found multiple opportunities to serve our area. We started hosting community cookouts; we provided all the food for free, had gospel singing, games, just a grand time to connect with those around us.

We offered our facilities for traveling medical clinics designed to reach and benefit the less fortunate.

We updated all of our vehicle fleet, trading in all of the now perpetually broken-down buses for much newer and nicer and more usable transit vans.

In all of this and so much more, our mindset was to rebuild our church's damaged reputation to such a degree that all the community around us would hold us in higher esteem than ever before. And just last week, as I write this, while doing an outreach to the local university, a gentleman of another ethnicity from across the county made his way to the table I was working and said, "Pastor, you don't know me, but I just wanted you to know that your church has a great reputation in the community. Thank you for all that you and your people do!"

That was and is worth more to me than all of the riches of the earth.

Pastor, if you want to survive your perfect storm long-term, do not stay as you are. Update and improve absolutely everything until all of the vestiges of the painful past are nothing but a distant memory, and all that is left is something shiny and new that still holds all of the proper biblical beliefs and behaviors of the old.

Chapter 24
The Sun Will Shine Again

In this last chapter, dear Pastor, please allow me to pour my heart out to you in the most positive way possible. Know that I have been where you are, I have felt what you feel, and I know how bad it is. But more importantly than that, please rest assured that if you will simply keep going and continue to do right, the sun will shine again.

No, I cannot guarantee you that your church will outgrow your split. I am quite confident that it stands extremely good odds to do so if you follow the principles laid forth in this book, but I cannot guarantee anything in that regard. I can tell you, though, that if you will continue to walk with the Lord, and if you will continue to be faithful, and if you will continue to do right, the sun will shine again.

Do you remember what God told Israel in some of the darkest of her dark days?

Jeremiah 29:11 *For I know the thoughts that I think toward you, saith the LORD, thoughts* *of peace, and not of evil, to give you an expected end.*

This is the same God that we still serve today.

From experience, I know that going through a church split is the most heart-wrenching thing you will likely ever endure. You had friends, best friends. They are now your mortal enemies, and you do not understand quite why. You gave so much of yourself to them and for them; you sacrificed and were there for them when they needed you the most. Now, they seem intent on trying to destroy you.

Your family is hurting. You see the tears and hear the sobbing on a nightly basis; you wonder if it will ever get better.

You are scared about the future. You do not know if your own finances will survive, let alone those of the church.

You wonder if your ministry will ever recover; you have prepared for it and trained for it and worked so hard in it, and now you wonder if it was all for naught.

I have been there. The sun will shine again.

I lost a lot of very good friends in our split. I have also regained quite a few of them as the years have gone on and the wounds have healed and forgiveness has been applied. I am actually now on better terms with some of them than ever before!

God also used our split, though, to solidify friendships that I did have beyond any possible human measure. Some of my dearest friends in life, when the chips were down, stood right by my side the entire way. I do not hesitate to say that I would willingly die for them at this point; those friendships were made utterly priceless to me as they endured the pressure of our storm alongside of me.

God also brought many new friends into my life, friends that I absolutely would not have had if our storm never occurred. New members have come to our church who have become as dear as family to me, people who came because God sent them to fill a void created by someone else who had left. I cannot imagine life without them, and I would not have them save for our storm.

The sun will shine again.

Our split gave us what I call "a holy desperation to win souls." When there are bunches of empty pews, one has abundant motivation to win the lost and bring them in! And because of this, we have gotten to experience the ultimate joy of a Christian on this side of heaven, seeing a huge number of people come to know Christ and have their lives transformed by Him.

We have experienced that joy in much greater measure on this side of the split than prior to our split.

The sun will shine again.

Pastors from near and far reached out to us during our storm, men with whom I was only dimly acquainted before it happened. They have become dear friends and co-laborers to me.

The sun will shine again.

I prayed before our split. But after it, my prayers were far more real and raw and desperate. And I do not shy from saying that I have seen far more specific prayers answered after our split than before it. My relationship with God is so much more now than it ever was before the storm.

The sun will shine again.

My children, who were no more than typical Sunday school tykes before everything happened, have seen their parents and their church come through the most horrible circumstances and yet remain joyful and vibrant. Because of that, all of my now adult children are still serving the Lord faithfully, and their relationship with Christ has a much greater depth than I would have thought possible at their young ages.

The sun will shine again.

All of your details may not be the same as were mine. All of your outcomes will likely not be the same as are mine. But the God of heaven prizes and honors faithfulness. And though your storm seems as drastic as that of Noah and every bit as long-lasting or longer, just as the sun shone again for him, it will shine again for you.

You can do it, Pastor; you can survive the perfect storm.